Tim Hoppey

Written by
Tim Hoppey

Illustrated by
Lori McElrath-Eslick

The Good
Fire Helmet

DAD

Alma Little
St Paul, Minnesota

The Good Fire Helmet. Text © 2010 Tim Hoppey. Illustrations © 2010 Lori McElrath-Eslick.
All rights reserved. Design by Andermax Studios.
Library of Congress Cataloging-in-Publication Data:
Hoppey, Tim.
The good fire helmet / written by Tim Hoppey ; illustrated by Lori McElrath-Eslick.
p. cm.
Summary: Six-year-old Christian believes that an old fire helmet makes him brave,
while his ten-year-old brother, Tommy, finds courage within himself,
especially when he needs it most.
ISBN 978-1-934617-06-9 (hardcover)
[1. Courage—Fiction. 2. Faith—Fiction. 3. Brothers—Fiction. 4. Helmets—Fiction.]
I. McElrath-Eslick, Lori, ill. II. Title.
PZ7.H7794 Goo 2010
[E]—dc22
2009031873

Printed in Canada. 1 2 3 4 5 6 7 8 9 10
Alma Little is an imprint of Elva Resa Publishing, St Paul, Minnesota
http://www.elvaresa.com

For Lauren and Tommy Dennis

Tommy was ten, and he no longer believed in the fire helmet. Christian was six. He still believed.

Whenever he had to go to the doctor to get a shot, Christian would first put on the fire helmet. He believed the fire helmet gave him the courage to get the shot without crying. With that big helmet falling down over his eyes, he wouldn't so much as flinch when the shot went into his arm.

The doctor would say to their mother, "That's a brave little fireman you've got there."

Most of the time the fire helmet sat upon the boys' dresser. It was a good fire helmet, not shiny and new, but sooty the way a fire helmet should be. Its leather was cracked and bent in such a way that you could see it had been worn during many heroic deeds. The number that had once been white was now so blackened it was hard to make out the 91, which was the number of the engine company where this helmet had worked.

Every night when their mother tucked them into bed, she kissed each boy goodnight. Then, before turning out the light, she kissed the top of the fire helmet and whispered a few words the boys couldn't hear.

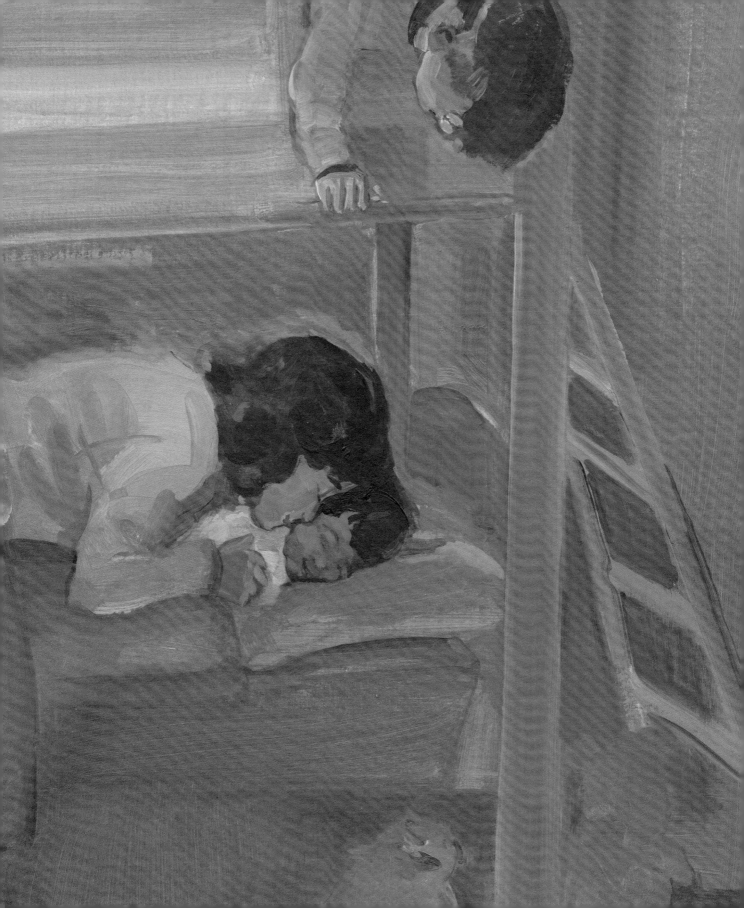

Tommy remembered the day when the chaplain had held this helmet before him and said, "This helmet has a good deal of courage in it. It's been down dark, smoky hallways and done many great deeds. As you get older, there will be days when you will need to be brave. Perhaps you won't believe you can do it. On those days, if you just touch your fingers to this fire helmet, its courage can be given to you. A good fire helmet has been known to do that."

Christian believed.

One night the shadows crept like tigers toward his bed. The next night the shadows circled like sharks.

"Make them go away, Tommy," he cried.

On those nights, Tommy got out of bed and walked across the room to the dresser. The fire helmet felt heavy when he lifted it, and heavier still when he placed it beside Christian's pillow for courage. After that, shadows in the bedroom didn't seem so scary anymore.

Of course, bravery is not just about getting a shot without crying or going to sleep in a room full of shadows. Sometimes you have to be brave just to get out of bed, eat breakfast, brush your teeth, and go off to school. That's how Tommy felt most mornings. It was hard to explain. He wasn't even sure what he was afraid of.

After school, Tommy often hiked to the creek where his father used
to take him fishing. There were secret fishing spots that only the two
of them knew about, where big fish could be caught if you knew
where to cast. Only, nowadays, Tommy didn't feel like bringing
along his tackle box and fishing pole.
   Christian tagged along wherever Tommy went.
   "Why are you wearing the fire helmet out here?" Tommy asked.

"Just in case there are tigers in the woods or sharks in the water," Christian said.

"There aren't any tigers in these woods," Tommy said. "And there aren't any sharks in the creek, either."

"Well, I've seen them," Christian said. "Look! A tiger!"

Tommy spun around.

"Made you look!" Christian laughed. Tommy didn't think it was funny.

"Come on, let's go home," Tommy said. Christian skipped along the path singing, the helmet bobbing up and down on his head. "It's a good thing we're not fishing today," Tommy said. "You're making so much noise you'd scare away all the fish."

Just then, the big fire helmet fell down over Christian's eyes and he tripped over a tree root. He tumbled down the bank and splashed into the creek.

When Christian popped to
the surface, the fire helmet
was missing from his head.
The water was so muddy that
at first the boys didn't see the
helmet.

"There it is!" Christian cried.

Before Tommy could tell him
not to, Christian stepped
farther out into the current.

The rushing water suddenly swept him away! Christian fought to keep his head above water. The creek was rain-swollen and running swiftly.

Tommy ran along the bank.

"Christian, swim to me!" he shouted.

Up ahead, there was a sturdy branch lying across the path. Tommy grabbed it and raced to get out in front of his brother.

Wrapping his leg around a stump, Tommy anchored himself to the bank. Then he cast the branch out into the creek as if he were fishing.

But the branch wasn't long enough. Unless Tommy stepped out farther into the creek, Christian wouldn't be able to catch hold of the branch.

The water was dark and churning. Tommy felt the current tugging at his leg. His father had taught him not to wade in past his knees when making a water rescue. And though the water was not yet that high on his leg, he hesitated.

To be brave when you're afraid of being brave is not an easy thing to do. That's how Tommy felt, anyway.

"You can lose a fish," his father used to say, "just don't lose faith."

The fire helmet floated past. Tommy could have reached out and touched it for courage, but he let the helmet pass him by. Instead, Tommy touched his fingers to his heart, struggling to find his own courage.

"You can do it," he told himself, as he took one big step out into the water.

Tommy reached way out over the water, farther than he ever thought he could.

"Grab hold of the branch!" he called to Christian.

"I can't!" Christian cried.

"You can do it!" Tommy told him. "You can do it!"

Christian was wide-eyed with fear. He gasped for air, and his arms flailed up and down.

Tommy shouted, "Courage, Christian! Just like Dad taught us!"

Then he braced himself and held tight to the branch as Christian grabbed hold.

Tommy struggled to pull Christian in. It felt like he had hooked a 40-pound catfish on a line. With his last tug, Tommy pulled Christian into his arms and hugged him tightly.

"The fire helmet!" Christian cried. "I lost the fire helmet!"

"That's okay," Tommy said. "We can both be brave without it."

On the way home, the boys found the fire helmet snagged in a tangle of weeds. Just its top was showing above the water, like the leathery shell of an old turtle.

"Eureka!" Christian shouted.

Tommy couldn't help but smile.

As they came through the door, their mother took one look at Christian and said, "All right, let's hear what happened."

Christian told their mother about falling into the creek and being swept away by the brown water. He told her all about the rescue and how daring Tommy had been in fishing him out. Tommy blushed to hear it.

That night, after their mother had tucked them into bed and kissed both boys goodnight, she walked to the dresser. The fire helmet sat there looking sooty and worn, and still a bit soggy, just the way a good fire helmet should. Before she could bend down to kiss the helmet, Tommy crossed the room and stood at her side.

"It sounds like you were really brave today," she said.

"I guess," Tommy said.

His mother reached over and mussed his hair. "You're just like your father," she said. "Courage comes to you when you need it most."

"I think I'll get up early and go fishing tomorrow," Tommy said. Then he touched his fingers to the fire helmet and whispered, "I know a place where big fish can be caught if you know where to cast."

For the past twenty-five years **TIM HOPPEY** has worked as a New York City firefighter stationed in Spanish Harlem. When he's not fighting fires, he runs summer rafting trips on the Delaware River for inner city boys. A lacrosse player, he enjoys throwing the ball around with his three adult children. Tim is the author of several children's books. He lives with his wife, Ellen, on Long Island.

An award-winning illustrator, **LORI McELRATH-ESLICK** has illustrated many children's books and her work has also appeared in magazines including *Highlights for Children*, *Ladybug*, and *National Wildlife*. She lives with her family in Michigan, where she enjoys painting, camping, swimming, and cross-country skiing.

ONE WAY

8/07

To my dutiful partners

ELMWOOD BRANCH

Jet
Likes flying at night
over strings of light,
tiny cars all aglow
on the roads below.

Tugboat

Small but tough,
he cheerily chugs
with the ships and barges
he *pushes* and *tugs*.

Speedboat

Sprays and splashes
in daring dashes
across the lake,
leaving waves
in his wake.

URGER

Ship
Dreams of being out at sea,
with schools of fish for company. . . .

Sailboat
Wind-catcher,
water-skipper,
white-sailed
wave-dipper.

Helicopter
Propellers whirring
on top of his head,
he can fly forward
or backward instead.

Car
Open the door,
jump in—*slam*.
Off we go
to the traffic jam.

Taxi

Knows the city—
her streets, her ways.
Enjoys a passenger
who's polite—and pays.

Fire Engine

Fast red truck
quickly arrives
to put out fires
and *save lives!*

Police Car

Lights flash, sirens wail.
Move aside, they say.
Someone's calling.
Someone needs me.
Help is on the way. . . .

Moving Van
Takes tables,
couches,
chairs,
beds too,
on the road
to someplace new!

Motor Home
Traveling house
likes to stop
to guzzle gas
like soda pop.

Motorcycle
Open and free.
No roof, no door.
Just wind and sun
and a rumbling *roar*.

Airplane

Up in the air
the metal bird sings,
Look at me.
I've got wings!

Freight Train

Boxcars, flatcars
clickety click click
carry corn, sugar, wheat,
steel, lumber, coal . . .
Click across the country roll
the boxcars, flatcars.
Come see! Come quick!
Clickety click click . . .

Pickup Truck

Climbs hills, hauls loads,
bounces over back roads.
You never know where to find him.
But don't worry.
He'll come home,
wagging his tailgate behind him.

Ice Skates
Spinning once,
twirling twice—
slipping, sliding *oops!*
on ice.

Sled
Runs down the hill
fast as he can go
till *bump*
he *thumps*
in a pile
of snow.

Skis

Down snowy slopes
the twin slats slide
in a slippery-dippery
rip-roaring ride.

Garbage Truck

Our street is clean . . .
he makes it possible
by gobbling trash,
anything tossable.

Mail Truck

Zips down the street
with letters and more.
Delivers . . . delivers . . .
door after door.

School Bus
Friendly fellow
dressed in yellow
greets his kids
with a *beep-beep* hello!

Ferris Wheel

Rolls around,
but doesn't roll away.
Stays on the ground
while her riders rise and sway.

Merry-Go-Round

Spins lions, zebras,
many a horse,
a jeweled giraffe . . .
and kids, of course!

Roller Coaster

Goes up slow,
but down fast *Oh!*
Like a scary dream,
makes us *scream.*

Wheelbarrow
Carries stones, dirt,
wood, a bush . . .
Just needs a push.

Red Wagon
Always getting
dragged behind,
filled and emptied . . .
Doesn't mind.

Lawn Mower

Chewing grass
is all she knows.
She never *moos,*
just mows and mows.

Ice Cream Truck

Chimes a welcome tune . . .
Ice-cold treats
for a hot afternoon!

Hot Air Balloon

Round, rising,
surprisingly bright,
she floats like a dream
in a feather-light flight. . . .

Skateboard

Just a board on wheels,
but full of *zizz*.
Jump on him
and away he'll *whiz*.

Scooter

Needs a hand.
Needs a foot.
Or else he'll have to
stay put.

Roller Skates

Lively boots
like how it feels
to *whoosh* around
on little wheels.

Bike and Trike

Bike teases Trike,
"Bet you wish you were me."
He thinks *two* wheels
are better than *three*!

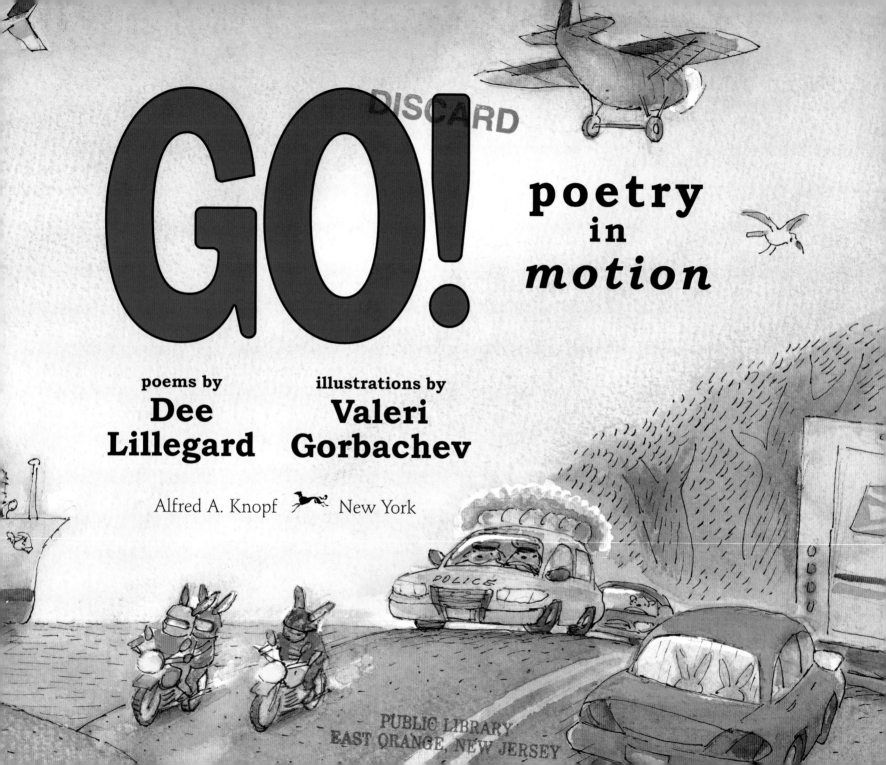

GO!

poetry in motion

**poems by
Dee
Lillegard**

**illustrations by
Valeri
Gorbachev**

Alfred A. Knopf · New York